Attention-Deficit Hyperactivity Disorder In Children: A Medication Guide

Hugh F. Johnston, M.D.

Rockston Ink
The Progressive Press

Madison Institute of Medicine

Preface

This revised booklet was written by Hugh F. Johnston, M.D., with helpful comments from Amy L. Rock, M.S.S.W., John H. Greist, M.D., James W. Jefferson, M.D., and J. Jay Fruehling, M.A. We are especially grateful for the careful editing and research work of Margaret G. Baudhuin, M.L.S., Bette L. Hartley, M.L.S., and Micki D. Thren of the Information Centers at the Madison Institute of Medicine located in Madison, Wisconsin. We extend our heartfelt gratitude to these individuals. We are also grateful to our patients, their families and our friends for reading drafts of this booklet and making important and useful suggestions.

Since the last edition of this booklet, both the American Academy of Child and Adolescent Psychiatry and the American Academy of Pediatrics have published standards for the diagnosis and treatment of Attention Deficit Hyperactivity Disorder (ADHD). New research has both illuminated the benefits of treatment and the impairments that result when ADHD is not treated. New medications and new formulations of old medications now allow more flexibility in treatment. Because of these advances, and because of increased public awareness, more children with ADHD are being appropriately diagnosed and treated. Children who would have once been left behind, today have better chances to succeed, both academically and socially.

Despite this progress, there is still much controversy and misunderstanding about ADHD. Many worry that ADHD is over-diagnosed, while others worry that ADHD is too often overlooked. Parents, in particular, wonder if medication treatment is truly the best course of action. The guiding principle behind this booklet is: *People make the best decisions when they have the best information.* Our goal is to present the most relevant information in a concise, understandable manner. We believe we have succeeded, but we are continuously striving to improve the quality of our publications and encourage readers to write us with their comments.

The authors have worked to ensure that all information in this booklet is accurate at the time of publication. As medical research and practice advance, some changes will undoubtedly occur. For this reason, and because human and mechanical errors sometimes occur, readers should follow the advice of a physician directly involved in their care or in the care of a member of their family.

Rockston Ink: The Progressive Press

Previous printing: April, 1999

Contents

What is the proper name for this disorder? How are children diagnosed as having ADHD? Behaviors that are supportive of childhood ADHD. Is there a specific test for ADHD? Can a child have just a little ADHD? Are there other causes for ADHD symptoms besides ADHD? How common is ADHD? What causes ADHD? Is ADHD inherited? Is ADHD a "chemical imbalance?" Can someone have ADHD and not be hyperactive? What are the complications of ADHD? Is there a cure for ADHD? Can ADHD be treated without medications? Can ADHD be controlled by a special diet? Have herbal treatments been proven safe and effective for ADHD? What else can be done to help a child with ADHD?

What do doctors need to know before prescribing medicine to treat ADHD? Why are medication names so confusing? Are laboratory tests necessary before starting medication treatment? How is the correct medication dose determined? What if a medication doesn't help? Which medications are used to treat ADHD? Are these medications approved by the U.S. Food and Drug Administration (FDA)? Can children take medication that is FDA approved for adults only? Which medication is "best?" Why don't stimulant medications make children with ADHD even more active? How does antidepressant medication help ADHD? When should an antidepressant be used to treat ADHD? Which is better, bupropion (Wellbutrin) or a tricyclic antidepressant (TCA)? When should clonidine (Catapres) or guanfacine (Tenex) be used to treat ADHD? Are there medical conditions that prohibit the use of medications?

Stimulant medications   20

What are the differences among stimulants? What are the beneficial effects of stimulants? Which stimulant is best for ADHD? How should stimulants be taken? Are laboratory tests needed before or during stimulant therapy? What are the usual doses and available pill sizes for each of the stimulant medications? Which side effects may occur during stimulant therapy? Are there delayed side effects from stimulants? Are there stimulant side effects for which a doctor should be contacted immediately? What are signs and symptoms of a stimulant overdose?

Tricyclic antidepressants (TCAs)   30

What are the beneficial effects of TCAs? What are the differences among TCAs? Which TCA is best for ADHD? How should TCAs be taken? What is the usual dose of a TCA? Do TCAs have side effects? Which side effects occur early in TCA therapy? Are there side effects from TCAs that may not occur right away? Are there TCA-related side effects for which a doctor should be contacted immediately? Are laboratory tests necessary during TCA treatment? What are signs and symptoms of a TCA overdose?

Bupropion (Wellbutrin, Zyban)   35

What are the beneficial effects of bupropion? What is the correct dose of bupropion ? How should bupropion be taken? Does bupropion have side effects? Which side effects occur early in bupropion therapy? Are there bupropion side effects which may not occur right away? Are there bupropion side effects for which a doctor should be contacted immediately? Are laboratory tests necessary during bupropion treatment? What are signs and symptoms of a bupropion overdose?

Clonidine (Catapres) and guanfacine (Tenex)   38

What are the beneficial effects of clonidine and guanfacine? How is clonidine or guanfacine therapy started? What are the correct doses of clonidine and guanfacine? How should clonidine or guanfacine be taken? Are any laboratory tests necessary during clonidine or guanfacine treatment? Which side effects occur early in clonidine or guanfacine therapy? Are there clonidine or guanfacine side effects that might not occur right away? Do clonidine or guanfacine have any serious side effects? How should clonidine or guanfacine treatment be stopped? What are signs and symptoms of a clonidine or guanfacine overdose?

Additional commonly asked questions   42

What should be done if a child skips a dose of medication? What should be done if a dose of medication is mistakenly taken twice? Do ADHD medications interact with other prescription medications? Do ADHD medications interact with over-the-counter medicines such as cough syrups or cold remedies? Can a child become addicted to stimulants? Can a child become addicted to the other medications (besides stimulants) used to treat ADHD? Can a child grow up to become a drug abuser because of stimulant treatment now? Do stimulants or other medications for ADHD ever stop working in a child? Shouldn't children and parents learn to overcome difficulties without drugs? Aren't stimulants over-prescribed? Can the long-term use of stimulants or other ADHD medications harm a child? If a child has severe ADHD, can several medications be used together? Can ADHD be treated with caffeine? Can a child taking a medication for ADHD participate in sports? What is the youngest age that a child can be treated with medication? Do children outgrow ADHD? Do adults suffer ADHD? How can someone learn all that is important about ADHD and its treatment?

Introduction

This guidebook is for:

Parents of children taking medications for ADHD
Parents considering medication treatment for their children with ADHD
Pediatricians, family practice physicians, and other doctors treating ADHD
Teachers and child care workers
Children and adolescents with attention problems considering medication
treatment
Other interested persons

It is a guide to understanding:

Attention-deficit hyperactivity disorder (ADHD)
How medications are used to treat ADHD
How medication therapy is started and continued
Which side effects could occur and how they can be managed

We hope it will help:

Maximize the benefits of appropriate medication treatment for ADHD
Minimize inappropriate medication therapy
Reduce treatment difficulties
Ensure the safe and effective use of medication to treat ADHD

What is attention-deficit hyperactivity disorder (ADHD)?

What is the proper name for this disorder? This disorder has had a variety of names over the years. Some of these include attention deficit disorder (ADD), attention-deficit disorder with hyperactivity (ADDH), hyperkinetic reaction of childhood, hyperkinetic syndrome, hyperactive child syndrome, minimal brain damage, minimal brain dysfunction, minimal cerebral dysfunction, and minor cerebral dysfunction. A few of these names imply that ADHD is due to brain damage. In fact, very few children with ADHD have ever suffered any type of brain damage. However, relatively little is known about the actual causes of this disorder.

Most of the names above were used before the systematic classification of mental disorders became a generally accepted practice. Today physicians most often use the *Diagnostic & Statistical Manual of Mental Disorders, Fourth Edition* (DSM-IV) as an aid in making a diagnosis. The DSM-IV term for this disorder is *Attention-Deficit/Hyperactivity Disorder* (ADHD) and is the term most widely used. In this booklet, we will use the abbreviation ADHD. To more accurately define the disorder, the DSM-IV further classifies ADHD into subtypes. These include:

Attention-Deficit/Hyperactivity Disorder, Combined Type. This subtype is the most commonly seen and describes children who are both hyperactive and also have short attention spans.

Attention-Deficit/Hyperactivity Disorder, Predominantly Inattentive Type. This subtype describes children who have very short attention spans, yet are not particularly hyperactive.

Attention-Deficit/Hyperactivity Disorder, Predominantly Hyperactive-Impulsive Type. This subtype describes children who are hyperactive yet have relatively normal attention spans.

Attention-Deficit/Hyperactivity Disorder, Not Otherwise Specified. This subtype is used for children who have atypical symptoms to a degree that none of the other subtypes are appropriate.

How are children diagnosed as having ADHD? A physician or psychologist usually makes the diagnosis, based on direct observation of the child's behavior, and on reports about the child's behavior gathered from parents and teachers. The diagnosis of ADHD is considered when a child exhibits a level of inattention, impulsivity, and hyperactivity that is substantially greater than would be expected of most children the same age. The age of the child must always be taken into consideration when making the diagnosis because younger children are normally more inattentive, impulsive, and active than older children. It is important to remember that most children are occasionally impulsive, inattentive, and overly active. The occasional occurrence of these behaviors does not warrant a diagnosis of ADHD.

Unlike most psychiatric diagnoses, ADHD usually does not have a specific time of onset. Most children diagnosed with ADHD have a history of being active and inattentive at a very early age, although the diagnosis is typically not made until the child is in school. This is because the ADHD symptoms usually do not cause problems until the child is required to sit still and pay attention in a classroom situation. As a rule, ADHD is *not* diagnosed *unless* the child's difficulties were at least partially apparent before age seven.

Another diagnosis that has some similarities to ADHD is bipolar disorder (manic-depression). In both disorders children commonly have symptoms of increased physical activity, rapid speech, and difficulties with social interactions. Unlike ADHD, bipolar disorder is usually cyclical, meaning that the problems wax and wane over time. Also, in bipolar disorder the most prominent feature is that the child has great difficulty regulating mood—even in the best of circumstances. These characteristics help distinguish it from ADHD. At times it can be difficult to differentiate between these two disorders, and it is best to consult with an expert if uncertainty exists. It is also possible to have both disorders at the same time. Estimates vary, but perhaps half of children with bipolar disorder also have ADHD.

In addition, there are a great number of other reasons why a child can be troubled with a short attention span and/or hyperactivity. Some of these include a depressed mood, an anxiety disorder, nervousness, physical illness, drug abuse, neglect, and child abuse. Each of these possibilities should be considered when evaluating a child for ADHD.

Behaviors that are supportive of childhood ADHD:

- Constant physical motion, such as twiddling fingers, tapping feet, playing with hair, bouncing up and down
- Difficulty remaining in one place
- Never walking, always running from place to place
- Physical recklessness or clumsiness; often falling due to running without paying attention to obstacles
- An inability to play quietly
- Talking excessively, or too loudly
- Frequently interrupting others, or attempting to answer questions before they have been completely asked
- Difficulty waiting
- Ignoring or forgetting directions only moments after they have been given
- Impulsiveness or open defiance
- Difficulty listening to what others have to say
- Failing to complete simple tasks on time, like getting dressed for school
- Often losing things such as books, toys, or pencils
- Often failing to recognize danger. For example, running across a busy street without looking or climbing into precarious places
- Becoming easily lost in unfamiliar surroundings
- Insensitivity to the pain of minor injuries
- Frequent frustration and impatience
- Unpredictable changes in emotional state
- Frequent and unexpected changes from one play activity to another

Ultimately, the diagnosis of ADHD is based upon a child's *behavior*. The diagnosis can be made with certainty only if the doctor has directly observed many of the behaviors listed above, or has reliable information from parents, teachers, or others who spend a substantial amount of time with the child. There are no specific blood tests or other laboratory tests which can be used to diagnose ADHD. It is important to stress that none of the specific behaviors used to make a diagnosis of ADHD are, by themselves, unusual. However, when these behaviors occur with enough frequency, consistency and severity that they significantly interfere with the child's functioning at home or school, ADHD should be considered.

Although children with ADHD can have difficulty in many life situations, they tend to have the most difficulty when they are expected to sit still and pay attention. For example, the behaviors of a child with ADHD may be indistinguishable from those of friends on the playground, but might become very disruptive when the child is asked to sit quietly in a classroom or church. Once again, it should be stressed that while many children have trouble sitting quietly, the child with ADHD has much more difficulty than a typical child of the same age.

At home, children with ADHD often have trouble remaining seated during meals, and if forced to remain seated, will tend to disrupt mealtime. They may do this by talking incessantly, wiggling in their seats, dropping their silverware on the floor, or playing with their food. Likewise, they are typically unable to sit through an entire television program without fidgeting, running around the room, or talking. Children with ADHD will intrude impulsively on other family members' activities or conversations, leading to considerable annoyance on the part of siblings or parents. Long automobile rides may be particularly difficult for children with ADHD (and their parents!).

At school, children with ADHD often resist following classroom routines. They may talk out of turn, leave their chairs without asking, intrude on other children, distract other children from their lessons, and appear inattentive. Frequently, schoolwork assignments are only partially finished, or are completed sloppily. When given several tasks to accomplish, these children have difficulty organizing their work and time. Teachers can become distressed by children with ADHD, particularly if there is more than one child with the disorder in the classroom.

Children with ADHD also have difficulty with peer relationships. Because of a poor attention span and impulsivity, they often fail to follow rules in structured games. Their intrusiveness and physical overactivity can lead to play that is too rough for the situation, resulting in accidents and injuries. Intruding inappropriately on other children's play activities can lead to fighting.

The specific problems that children with ADHD encounter depend, in part, on their age. Younger children are more likely to have difficulty with physical overactivity, while older children and adolescents are more likely to have problems related to poor attention span. Older children can often control physical overactivity to a socially acceptable degree, but may appear irresponsible, messy, or careless. Because of poor attention spans, they often fail to complete projects, or complete them in very hasty and impulsive ways. Impulsiveness may also cause problems when children divert their attention from commitments and responsibilities to engage in pleasurable but nonproductive activities. For example, a child with ADHD walking to school can become so distracted by interesting birds, insects, clouds, or personal thoughts that all sense of time is lost, and tardiness is the result.

Is there a specific test for ADHD? No, there are no specific blood tests, brain scans, or psychological tests that can establish a diagnosis of ADHD with certainty. This comes as a surprise to many, given the enormous technological advances in modern medicine. While there are tests that can measure certain aspects of a child's ability to pay attention, a diagnosis of ADHD is ultimately based upon how the child's behaviors affect his success in school and at home. If a case is unusually complex, most primary care doctors will request a consultation with a specialist such as a child neurologist or child psychiatrist to ensure that the diagnosis is correct.

In some cases doctors will recommend tests to help clarify a complex case or to rule out certain conditions that can mimic ADHD. For example, psychological tests are used if there is suspicion of a learning disorder and certain blood tests are used if there is concern about thyroid disease.

Can a child have just a little ADHD? Yes, the severity of ADHD symptoms can range from mild to severe. It is similar, in this respect, to other conditions such as obesity. Most people who have a few extra pounds would not be given a diagnosis of obesity. On the other hand, if someone is one hundred pounds overweight, a diagnosis of obesity is perfectly clear. In both obesity and ADHD there are "gray zones" where experts can honestly disagree about whether a diagnosis is appropriate.

In cases of mild to moderate ADHD symptoms, the question of diagnosis hinges on impairment. If the symptoms result in significant problems at school or home, then a diagnosis and treatment may be warranted. But if the symptoms only result in a minor inconvenience, then there is little reason to diagnose ADHD.

Are there other causes for ADHD symptoms besides ADHD? Yes! Many other psychiatric disorders can "mimic" ADHD. For example, most children who are suffering from depression or bipolar illness have difficulty paying attention. Thus, these mood disorders can resemble ADHD. In a similar fashion, many children who are troubled by anxiety can appear to be inattentive when they are actually attending to their own worries or anxiety. They can also be quite physically active because of their nervousness. Physical illnesses can also produce symptoms that closely resemble the overactivity commonly seen in ADHD; one example is lead poisoning. This is why children who are significantly troubled with ADHD-like symptoms should have a medical evaluation to rule out other causes. A medical evaluation is especially important if the ADHD symptoms are new or have suddenly worsened.

Occasionally, certain medications such as asthma medications or over-the-counter cold remedies can produce behavioral changes that mimic ADHD. This can also happen when children abuse drugs.

How common is ADHD? Estimates of the number of children affected by this disorder vary. In the United States perhaps as many as two to five percent of children have ADHD and it is from two to five times more common in boys than girls.

What causes ADHD? The exact causes of ADHD are still unknown. Occasionally, the disorder develops following a brain injury or a medical disease. Sometimes a disorganized and chaotic family life or a history of child abuse seem to be a contributing factor. ADHD quite frequently occurs along with other disorders such as tic disorders, learning disorders, cerebral palsy, or other neurological problems. This makes determining a cause very difficult. Many parents are uncomfortable not having a clear explanation for why their child has ADHD. Nevertheless, the majority of children diagnosed with ADHD have no known history of brain injury and come from intact supportive families.

This means that ADHD probably has many different causes. A useful analogy is to compare ADHD to coughing. A person suffering from a cough may have an underlying problem with allergies, pneumonia, lung cancer, or just a common cold. Similarly, a child suffering from ADHD may have any number of underlying problems too. Today, we know much less about the underlying causes of ADHD than we do about the underlying causes of coughing, but progress is being made.

When a child has a specific cause for his ADHD symptoms, such as a brain injury, the technically correct diagnosis is "mental disorder due to brain injury" or "ADHD-type symptoms secondary to brain injury." In reality, this practice is not always followed because it is cumbersome.

It has been theorized that ADHD may not be a disorder in the usual sense of the word, but rather a result of the normally wide range of variability inherent in the human race. One of the great strengths of the human race is the enormous variability that exists from person to person. Because of this variability we have individuals who make great professional football players, others who are well suited to be accountants, and still others who are endowed with the ability to become virtuoso violinists. These theorists suggest that perhaps those with ADHD might represent one aspect of this variability—an aspect that is particularly ill-suited for sitting quietly in a schoolroom.

This theory seems plausible for several reasons. Children with ADHD don't appear to be "ill" or "suffering" unless they are attempting to do certain types of tasks, e.g., following a schedule, quietly paying attention, remembering details. Also, ADHD is very common compared to many other "illnesses." And lastly, ADHD-like individuals are found in many species of social animals. For example, most flocks of crows have one or two birds that are especially distractible and noisy. These birds serve as "sentinels" to alert the rest of the flock to danger. Whether this interesting theory turns out to be true or not does not change the fact that, in today's world, children with ADHD often struggle with very significant impairments.

Is ADHD inherited? Using complicated statistical analyses, scientists have determined that about 80% of ADHD *symptoms* result from inheritance while the other 20% result from other factors. This is a generalization that will vary considerably from individual to individual. Just as we have all known of families in which every member has a very prominent nose, there are also families in which everyone has prominent ADHD. None-the-less, the majority of ADHD cases are not nearly so clear cut. Recently, the sequencing of the human genetic code was completed, and this holds great promise for eventually bringing to light the details of how and when ADHD is inherited.

In many instances, one or more relatives (including parents) of a child with ADHD also has the disorder, although it may never have been diagnosed or treated. It was once believed that only children could have ADHD; although we now know that the disorder often persists into adulthood, continuing to cause significant distress and impairment. When a child is diagnosed with ADHD, we now recommend that any relatives with similar symptoms also consider undergoing an evaluation.

Is ADHD a "chemical imbalance?" Perhaps. The idea that there are chemicals in the brain that become "out of balance" and lead to ADHD is an interesting one, but there is little scientific proof of this. Experts *are* in agreement that since medication is often very helpful, it must change some aspect of brain functioning. Whether this means a child has a "chemical imbalance" remains to be seen. Over the past several years, new technologies have emerged that are allowing scientists to measure brain functioning more precisely. Some examples include positron emission tomography, commonly known as "PET" scans, and functional magnetic resonance imaging, which is sometimes abbreviated as *f*MRI. These technologies hold great promise for understanding how and why ADHD occurs, although this research is still in an early stage of development.

Can someone have ADHD and not be hyperactive? Occasionally, a child is identified who has significant attention span problems but very few of the "over-activity" behaviors typically seen in ADHD. The technical term for this is *Attention-Deficit Hyperactivity Disorder, Predominantly Inattentive Type.* It is unknown how common this form of ADHD is, because these children rarely cause problems for teachers or parents and, therefore, are less likely to be seen as needing treatment. It has been speculated that girls may be more likely to have ADHD of this type. However, these individuals, regardless of their gender, often benefit from treatment, particularly in regard to their schoolwork.

What are the complications of ADHD? One common complication of ADHD is school failure. Because these children are physically very active and have difficulty maintaining attention, they often miss important concepts and can easily fall behind in their schoolwork. Once they are behind, they usually have great difficulty catching up because they lack the sustained, focused attention needed to do so. School difficulties can contribute to a negative self-image, causing these children to believe they are "stupid." If identified by school staff as "trouble makers," children with ADHD may be expelled or otherwise denied the support and special programming they need. This can lead to an inadequate development of social skills, leading in turn to rejection by peers and low self-esteem.

Another complication is a highly increased risk of drug and alcohol abuse. Children with untreated ADHD have more than double the risk of substance abuse compared to unaffected children. Recent research has shown that medication treatment greatly reduces this risk. Researchers speculate that the high risk of substance abuse results from the unhappiness and repeated failures experienced by these children. Effective treatment may allow children with ADHD to experience more success and thus make it less likely that they will turn to drug abuse.

Is there a cure for ADHD? There is no known cure for ADHD. Many children will improve considerably by the time they enter adolescence, but a substantial number of children with ADHD continue to have attention problems throughout their teen years and on into adulthood (see page 47). While there is presently no known cure, appropriate treatment almost always enables those with ADHD to lead productive and satisfying lives.

Can ADHD be treated without medications? Children with ADHD, particularly those with mild symptoms, can respond to carefully structured and organized classroom and social situations. When designing an educational program for children with ADHD, there are a number of important principles and techniques that can help each child succeed.

1. *Establish close, non-punitive supervision.* Positive adult feedback can help control and redirect an ADHD child's activity toward successfully completing educational assignments. Since adult input must be repeated frequently, it should not be done in a punitive manner or the child will soon become demoralized and oppositional, or simply quit trying. Such close supervision requires a favorable student/teacher (or aide) ratio that unfortunately is not always available. It is important that children with ADHD not be "over controlled." Many behaviors such as wiggling, talking to oneself, or being impatient are not necessarily detrimental to learning and should be tolerated as much as possible.

2. *Structured classroom activities.* Children with ADHD quickly become disorganized and disruptive when they find themselves in an unstructured environment. High levels of noise or activity in a minimally structured "open" classroom can aggravate hyperactive behaviors. Teacher expectations should be clear and predictable, and it is helpful if there is a consistent classroom routine. Frequent breaks to allow

children with ADHD to release physical energy may increase their ability to stay focused on educational tasks. Whenever possible, physical activity should be incorporated into learning activities.
3. *Supervised play activity.* Close supervision should also be extended to the school's playground and lunchroom. Without such supervision, the extreme physical activity, impulsivity and intrusiveness of children with ADHD can lead to negative interactions with peers. With help from adults, these children can usually enjoy positive friendships which will enhance their self-esteem.

The same behavioral principles applied at school can be used in the home. However, these techniques require a considerable amount of the parents' time, patience and energy. Many communities have valuable parent training classes and support groups. In addition, self-help books are useful in enhancing parents' ability to raise children with ADHD (see the suggested non-technical readings, page 49).

Unfortunately, even after carefully structuring both school and home activities, most children with ADHD will still be unable to function well. A recent large study comparing medication and behavioral treatment found that even very elaborate and carefully designed behavioral programs have a much smaller effect than optimum medication treatment. Thus, medication should be considered for most children with ADHD.

Can ADHD be controlled by a special diet? This question is raised by many parents who believe their children become overly active after eating specific foods, especially those containing sugar or dyes. While carefully controlled studies have not shown special diets to be effective treatments for ADHD, clinical experience suggests that a few children *seem* affected by certain foods.

Another theory was that refined sugar and food additives made children hyperactive and inattentive. As a result, parents were encouraged to stop serving children foods containing artificial flavorings, preservatives, and sugars. However, this theory, too, came under question. In 1982, the National Institutes of Health (NIH), the Federal agency responsible for biomedical research, held a major scientific conference to discuss the issue. After studying the data, the scientists concluded that the restricted diet seemed to help only about 5 percent of children with ADHD, mostly either young children or children with food allergies.

Although we do not recommend a particular diet for all children with ADHD, and battles over food can be counterproductive, there is usually little harm in restricting particular foods if they appear to cause problems. None-the-less, because stimulants tend to make children less hungry, it may not be wise to restrict favorite foods, since the extra calories may be needed. Also, because some children with ADHD can be finicky eaters, they should take a multivitamin daily to ensure adequate nutrition. If a child's behavior seems strongly influenced by a particular food, a physician should be consulted. This is because in rare instances, a child can have an underlying medical problem that results in discomfort after eating certain foods. This discomfort can lead to misbehaviors that can mimic those found in ADHD.

Have herbal treatments been proven safe and effective for ADHD? No. Every few years we see an aggressive marketing campaign promoting some "newly discovered" herbal remedy for ADHD that is claimed to be better than any of the "harsh chemicals" offered by doctors. Thus far, none of these claims have been supported by sound research. Instead of research, those who make such claims almost always use unsubstantiated testimonials in an effort to lend credibility to their statements.

Many people are of the opinion that herbal remedies are safer than manufactured medications because they "come from nature." This idea has some intuitive appeal, but the reality is that many substances that come from nature are significantly toxic—tobacco is but one example. Even if the herbal substance itself is safe, there have been many problems with contamination during compounding and packaging. In particular, heavy metal contamination (lead, cadmium, and others) has happened repeatedly.

Because of these problems, we discourage the use of herbal medicine for the treatment of ADHD. If a parent has a strong desire to pursue this option, we recommend thoroughly investigating any product before giving it to a child. We also recommend that patients only use herbal products that are purchased from a major chain (such as Walmart or Walgreens). While not an absolute guarantee of safety, large corporations are probably less likely to stock contaminated herbal preparations.

We particularly discourage using any herbal preparations purchased through mail-order catalogues or through the Internet. Although there are almost certainly reputable organizations that use these venues, it is almost impossible to tell who is reputable and who is not.

What else can be done to help a child with ADHD? Children with additional difficulties such as low self-esteem, academic problems, or family discord can be helped by other types of intervention. For example, those with low self-esteem may benefit from individual or group psychotherapy that is focused upon enhancing individual self-esteem. Children who have fallen far behind in their schoolwork will need extra help to catch up. This extra help can take the form of special tutoring sessions, additional classes, or simply additional attention and involvement by the parents in the child's homework.

Family discord such as divorce or alcoholism, or a medically ill parent is a serious matter for any child, but particularly for a child with ADHD. These children may have already stretched their coping mechanisms to the limit in attempting to manage problems associated with their disorder. Therefore, parents should honestly examine the physical and mental health of their family, and not hesitate to seek additional professional help if it is needed. A doctor can provide information about resources available in the community to help with a wide variety of family issues.

Medications: an overview

What do doctors need to know before prescribing medicine to treat ADHD? Doctors typically gather a great deal of information before prescribing a medication. Their questions are usually focused on the following areas:

The child's medical history. Does the child have other medical conditions? For example, parents might be asked about epilepsy, allergies, asthma, or diabetes. Does the child currently take other medications? This information can help the doctor choose an appropriate medication and can also help prevent side effects.

The family history. The doctor will want to know if there is a family history of psychiatric illness, including ADHD, anxiety, depression, and alcoholism. The symptoms of several psychiatric disorders can mimic those of ADHD, so family history may help to clarify the diagnosis. Parents should be sure to inform the doctor about any family history of tics or abnormal body movements of any kind (see page 28 for description), because this information often affects the doctor's medication choice.

The child's developmental history. The doctor may ask about the child's behavior as an infant or toddler. Did talking begin on schedule? Was the child a fussy or difficult baby? Were sleep patterns regular? Was overactivity ever a problem as an infant? ADHD often develops at an early age. Knowing how long a child has had problems, and the severity of them, will help the doctor make an accurate diagnosis and decide which treatments are appropriate.

The child's school history. How is the child performing academically or behaving at school? Has the child failed any grades? Is the child in a class for the emotionally/behaviorally disturbed or learning disabled? The doctor may wish to contact the school directly to ask personnel to complete behavioral rating questionnaires. School personnel can provide information about how the child functions in settings that are especially difficult for those with ADHD. Gathering information from parents and school personnel about how the child is doing in school helps ensure that a correct diagnosis is made. The doctor may also ask teachers to repeat behavioral ratings once the child starts taking a medication to help determine how well it is working.

This list of questions is not intended to be absolutely complete, but it gives some idea of what the doctor may want to know about a child and family before beginning treatment for ADHD. The main point is to inform the doctor about any medical conditions, current or past medications, and the family's history of medical or psychiatric problems. If there is uncertainty about whether a particular fact should be mentioned, bring it up anyway. For example, over-the-counter medication use, herbal medicines, or dietary substances should all be mentioned. Without providing complete information, the safety and effectiveness of the doctor's care could be reduced.

Why are medication names so confusing? The main reason for the confusion is that medications have at least two names—a generic name, and a brand name (sometimes several brand names). This is actually true for many things besides medications. "Kleenex" is a brand name, while "facial tissues" is a generic name. "Pepsi" and "Coke" are brand names while "carbonated cola drink" is the generic name. It is common knowledge that Kleenex and facial tissues are the same thing, so there is little confusion. But when it comes to medications, the words may be unfamiliar and difficult to pronounce. For example, most people don't immediately recognize that Cylert is the same as pemoline.

In this booklet we have done several things to try to reduce the confusion. Brand names will be in bold typeface and generic names will be in italics. Thus it should be clear that **Kleenex** is a brand name and *facial tissues* a generic name. When it seems appropriate, we will mention both names together, typically with the brand name in parenthesis, i.e., *facial tissues* (**Kleenex**). We have also included two tables that list both the generic and brand names—one for stimulant medications on page 20, and one for tricyclic antidepressant medications on page 31. If these names are unfamiliar, you may want to fold the page corners so that you can refer back to them easily.

Are laboratory tests necessary before starting medication treatment?
Sometimes laboratory tests are appropriate before starting a medication. Which tests are performed depends, in part, upon the age of the child and the particular medication being used. These laboratory tests are discussed in further detail in the sections that follow on each specific class of medication.

How is the correct medication dose determined? The dose of a medication must always be individualized for the child. There is no simple rule that determines a "correct" dose. However, an overriding principle regarding medication therapy is that children should be treated with the amount of medication that produces a satisfactory result and that doesn't produce unpleasant side effects. Dosing approaches are also discussed in greater detail in the sections that describe the specific classes of medication.

What if a medication doesn't help? The first step is to discuss the situation with your doctor. A medication may not be helpful for a wide variety of reasons. For example, the dose may be too low, or there may be unpleasant side effects, or it may not be working simply because of the uniqueness of each child. If a particular medication isn't working, the doctor may suggest increasing the dose or switching to an alternative drug. One commonly overlooked reason why a medication isn't working is that the child has secretly not been taking it! Of course, medication treatment in children should always be carefully supervised by an adult. But even with such supervision, a few children will successfully avoid taking a medication by hiding it in their mouths and spitting it out later.

Which medications are used to treat ADHD? There are three classes of medication commonly used to treat ADHD:

1) Stimulant medications (see Table I, page 20)
2) Certain antidepressant medications (see Table II, page 31)
3) Certain blood pressure medications (see page 38)

The stimulant medications are by far the most commonly prescribed, simply because they work well, have a long history of safety, and rarely produce troubling side effects. Other medications are less often used, but their use is important to consider when stimulants haven't been effective, or have caused unpleasant side effects. Each class of medication is discussed in greater detail in the sections that follow.

When the three classes of commonly used medications identified above fail, other medications are occasionally prescribed. Some examples of these medications include: *divalproex* (**Depakote**), *fluoxetine* (**Prozac**), *haloperidol* (**Haldol**), *risperidone* (**Risperdal**), *modafinil* (**Provigil**) and many others. Because they are used so rarely for ADHD, these medications are not discussed in this booklet.

Are these medications approved by the U.S. Food and Drug Administration (FDA)? Yes, although only the stimulants are specifically approved for the treatment of ADHD in children and adults. Even though the non-stimulant medications discussed in this booklet are approved for treatment of other conditions, it is perfectly legal and acceptable to use them for ADHD. Many medications are used for a variety of conditions beyond their original intended purpose.

Can children take medication that is FDA approved for adults only? Yes, federal regulations give doctors wide latitude in prescribing medications to children. Because of the difficulties and expense involved in doing research on children, many drug companies only pursue FDA approval of medicines for adults. When a medication has FDA approval for use in adults only, the drug company may not market it as a treatment for children. The company is also required to include a statement in the official product information similar to the following: "The safety and effectiveness of this medication in children is unknown."

Parents may be understandably alarmed to read such statements about a medication that their child is taking every day. This is unfortunate because in reality, there usually is considerable information about medication safety and effectiveness in children. We encourage parents to discuss this issue with their child's doctor whenever a medication is prescribed that does not have FDA approval for use in children.

Which medication is "best?" Even though the stimulant medications are considered the first-line drug treatment of ADHD, no single medication, or even class of medication, should be viewed as "best" for the treatment of all children with ADHD. The principal reason that so many different medications are used to treat this disorder is that there is tremendous variation from child to child regarding symptoms, medication response, and side effects. What really matters is which of these medications works best for the individual child being considered.

For the majority of children with uncomplicated ADHD, one of the stimulant medications discussed in the following pages will be the "best." Occasionally, stimulants either simply don't work or produce objectionable side effects. An alternative medication would then be a better choice for that particular child.

In addition, ADHD is sometimes complicated by other psychiatric symptoms such as mood or anxiety problems. In such cases, the "best" medication would be the one that helps both the ADHD symptoms *and* the mood or anxiety problems.

Why don't stimulant medications make children with ADHD even more active? It was once thought that stimulant medications produced a paradoxical effect in individuals with ADHD because they seemed to slow children down instead of "stimulating" them. It is now known that stimulants decrease physical activity and increase attention span in most individuals, regardless of whether or not they have ADHD. The term "stimulant" here is used in the medical sense, meaning that these medications interfere with sleep; it does not mean that these medications "speed people up."

To add to the confusion, some people (rarely those with ADHD) abuse stimulant medications by taking very high doses and/or injecting them into their veins. A commonly used street name for drugs of this type is "speed." When stimulants are abused in this way they typically produce a sensation of euphoria and excitement. Even at small doses, some adults report a mild sensation of euphoria. However, at doses used to treat their ADHD, children rarely experience euphoria or excitement from these medications.

How does antidepressant medication help ADHD? No one knows for sure. However, it is known that only those antidepressants which act upon a group of brain chemicals called adrenergic neurotransmitters treat ADHD effectively. The class of medications called tricyclic antidepressants (TCAs) as well as *bupropion* (**Wellbutrin**) have adrenergic effects and are used to treat ADHD. These particular antidepressants slightly change the way the brain uses certain chemicals and these changes are beneficial to people with ADHD. This is currently an area of active research.

When should an antidepressant be used to treat ADHD? Although stimulants are usually the first choice of medications used to treat ADHD, there are several reasons why an antidepressant medication might work better than a stimulant. Each of these is discussed below.

When stimulant medications produce objectionable side effects. Some children cannot take stimulant medications because of side effects. For a few particularly sensitive children, nervousness, loss of appetite, tics, or insomnia can become severe, making an alternative drug a useful consideration.

When stimulant medications simply fail to work. Occasionally, for reasons that are not fully understood, stimulant medications simply don't work. While this is uncommon, it does happen, and alternative medications are sometimes effective when stimulants have failed. Usually, alternative medications are considered *after* a child has tried two or three stimulant medications without success.

When symptoms of depression or anxiety are also present. As previously noted, ADHD-like symptoms can sometimes be due to psychiatric disorders other than ADHD. ADHD can also occur along with another psychiatric disorder. In these situations, a single antidepressant medication can sometimes treat both the ADHD symptoms as well as additional mood or anxiety problems.

Which is better, *bupropion* **(Wellbutrin) or a tricyclic antidepressant (TCA)?** It depends on the needs of the child. The TCAs are often much less expensive and can help control anxiety symptoms while *bupropion* tends to have fewer side effects. Many children who cannot take a stimulant because it makes them feel too anxious will have the same difficulty with *bupropion* and a TCA may be a better choice. On the other hand, if a child did not have success with a stimulant because of a low mood and irritability, *bupropion* may be a better choice. The TCAs are further discussed beginning on page 30 and *bupropion* on page 35.

When should *clonidine* **(Catapres) or** *guanfacine* **(Tenex) be used to treat ADHD?** As noted above, some children either do not have a satisfactory result or have troublesome side effects from stimulant treatment. When this happens, an alternative medication is usually considered. *Clonidine* **(Catapres)** and *guanfacine* **(Tenex)** are two very similar medicines originally developed to control high blood pressure. Although they have not been as thoroughly studied, many physicians believe that *clonidine* and *guanfacine* are especially helpful for ADHD children who are extremely hyperactive or aggressive. Also, because both of these medications tend to produce some sedation, they may be particularly helpful for children with ADHD who have sleep-related problems. These medications are further discussed beginning on page 38.

Are there medical conditions that prohibit the use of medication? There are very few medical conditions that actually prohibit the use of medications for ADHD although many conditions warrant some caution. Certain kinds of glaucoma (an eye condition that is very rare in children) can be aggravated by stimulants. Should eye problems appear while taking stimulant medication, the medication should be stopped and a doctor contacted without delay.

Children with serious heart disease may experience an increase in chest pain when taking any medication for ADHD. If your child has a heart condition, this should be discussed with your doctor prior to beginning stimulant therapy.

Some children with epilepsy may have more frequent seizures when taking medication. In other cases, medication may actually reduce the frequency of seizures. If your child has epilepsy, or has had it in the past, discuss this with the doctor before beginning medication. Children who have had a brief seizure as an infant, due to a high fever (called a febrile seizure), do not have any increased risk of seizures from stimulant medication.

Many tic disorders including Tourette's disorder can be aggravated by stimulant medication (see page 28). Unfortunately tic disorders and ADHD often occur together, complicating the treatment of ADHD. In these cases, it is best to see a specialist who is familiar with both disorders. Many children with tic disorders (including Tourette's) can take stimulants, but this may require an adjustment in the medication used to treat the tics.

Although very rare, galactosemia deserves special mention. Perhaps as many as 80% of children with this disorder have ADHD, or ADHD-like symptoms. Children with galactosemia become gravely ill from even microscopic amounts of galactose, a substance commonly used as a filler in many medications. Any medication being considered for these children must be carefully researched to ensure that it does not contain galactose or related compounds (such as lactose).

When a child has another health condition that requires a medication, there is a possibility it will interact with the medication used to treat ADHD. Serious interactions are uncommon, but always inform your child's doctor(s) about all of the medications before combining drugs. As an added precaution, it is wise to discuss this with your pharmacist as well.

Stimulant medications

Even though there are only a few stimulant medications in current use, the drug companies apply different techniques in the manufacture of pills, resulting in fourteen brands. Depending on the technique used (and the medication itself), some brands act more quickly than others, and some have a longer duration of action than others. The table below lists the brand name, the generic name, whether the onset of action is rapid or delayed, and the approximate duration of action.

Table I: Stimulants*

Brand Name	Generic Name	Onset of Action	Duration of Action
Adderall	d, l -amphetamine	rapid	4-6 hours
Adderall XR	d, l -amphetamine	rapid	10-12 hours
Concerta	methylphenidate	rapid	10-14 hours
Cylert	pemoline	rapid	12+ hours
Dexedrine	dextroamphetamine	rapid	4-6 hours
Dexedrine Spansules	dextroamphetamine	delayed	6-8 hours
Dextrostat	dextroamphetamine	rapid	4-6 hours
Focalin	dexmethylphenidate	rapid	2-4 hours
Metadate CD	methylphenidate	rapid	6-8 hours
Metadate ER	methylphenidate	delayed	6-8 hours
Methylin	methylphenidate	rapid	2-4 hours
Methylin ER	methylphenidate	delayed	6-8 hours
Ritalin	methylphenidate	rapid	2-4 hours
Ritalin SR	methylphenidate	delayed	6-8 hours

*In addition to the medications listed in the table, there are also generic preparations of these stimulants that do not have a brand name.

What are the differences among stimulants? There are currently four stimulant medications (in a variety of brands) being used to treat ADHD in the United States. The most frequently prescribed stimulant is methylphenidate (**Concerta, Focalin, Metadate, Methylin, Ritalin**). Also quite commonly prescribed are the amphetamine medications which include dextroamphetamine (**Dexedrine, DextroStat**), and d, l -amphetamine (**Adderall**). There is also a uniquely long-acting stimulant medication, pemoline (**Cylert**), which is now rarely prescribed because of its potential to cause liver damage.

Methylphenidate, dexmethylphenidate and the *amphetamines* are similar in overall effectiveness, and many children respond similarly to any of these medications. About 30% however, respond preferentially to either a *methylphenidate* or an *amphetamine*, but not to both. Other than actually taking the medications, there is no way to tell which one will work best. Thus, if one stimulant is unsatisfactory, either because of side effects or lack of therapeutic effect, the doctor will often recommend another.

There are very few differences between *methylphenidate-based* and *amphetamine-based* medications. Their duration of effectiveness can vary considerably depending on the specific preparation. The beneficial effects of each typically begins within twenty minutes of taking a dose. Because of the difficulties inherent in multiple daily dosing of medication, the pharmaceutical industry has developed several longer acting preparations of stimulant medication that allow once daily dosing. Each of these is discussed in the following sections.

In 1996 the stimulant preparation **Adderall** became available. **Adderall** is a combination medication that contains both *dextroamphetamine* and *levoamphetamine*. The difference between *dextroamphetamine* and *levoamphetamine* is analogous to the difference between your right and left hand; they are identical except that one is the mirror-image of the other. In the case of **Adderall**, this difference may have some importance. The left-hand version of *amphetamine* (*levoamphetamine*) has slightly different effects compared to the right-hand version (*dextroamphetamine*). Thus, because **Adderall** contains *levoamphetamine*, it may have slightly different effects as compared to *dextroamphetamine* alone. Here, the generic term for **Adderall** is abbreviated as *d, l -amphetamine*.

In 2002 a *dexmethylphenidate* preparation, **Focalin**, was introduced. Other *methylphenidate* preparations contain both *dexmethylphenidate* and *levomethylphenidate* in equal amounts. Again, *dexmethylphenidate* and *levomethylphenidate* are mirror images of each other just as is the case with *dextroamphetamine* and *levoamphetamine*.

Unlike *amphetamine*, the left-hand version of *methylphenidate*, *levomethylphenidate,* is an <u>inactive</u> <u>substance</u>: it has neither benefits, nor side effects. Thus, **Focalin** is very similar to other *methylphenidate* preparations (such as **Ritalin**) with the exception that the equivalent dose of **Focalin** is exactly half the **Ritalin** dose. This is because the inactive *levomethylphenidate* component is not present. There is no evidence that **Focalin** works any differently than **Ritalin** or generic equivalents.

With the exception of *pemoline* (**Cylert**), all the stimulant medications are classified as Schedule-II controlled substances by the U.S. Drug Enforcement Agency (DEA). This is because they have the potential to be abused. To help reduce the chance of abuse, they can only be obtained in a one-month supply at a time, with a written prescription from a physician.

Pemoline (**Cylert**) has less potential for abuse and is classified as a Schedule-IV controlled substance. This means that prescriptions with refills of up to six months may be issued, and physicians may also telephone prescriptions to the pharmacy. *Pemoline* has a long duration of effectiveness (greater than 12 hours) and a slightly different side effect profile than the other stimulants. For example, *Pemoline* is less likely to cause the emotional instability, called "behavioral rebound," that is seen occasionally with the shorter-acting stimulants (see page 27). On the negative side, *pemoline* can cause serious liver problems. While this is a rare occurrence, there have been fatalities. Blood tests are therefore necessary to ensure that the liver is functioning well. Parents should also be aware of the symptoms of liver problems including persistent nausea, vomiting, abdominal pain, loss of appetite, or change in skin color.

In 1999 the primary company that manufactures *pemoline*, Abbott Laboratories, strongly recommended that blood tests for liver functioning be done every other week. Because this is very inconvenient, expensive, and unpleasant, *pemoline* is now rarely prescribed. Some physicians feel that this recommendation is excessively cautious and do not insist that blood tests be done so frequently. If your child is prescribed *pemoline*, it is important to have an in-depth discussion about this issue with your physician.

What are the beneficial effects of stimulants? In general, these medications increase both alertness and the ability to focus attention more easily. They also decrease distractibility and hyperactivity. This enables a child with ADHD to function at a level much closer to his or her true potential than is possible without medication. Stimulant medications do not guarantee that a child will perform better in school, or be more successful socially. However, the beneficial effects are dramatic for children who have the potential to succeed, but repeatedly fail because their ADHD symptoms interfere.

Which stimulant is best for ADHD? Because children often have an individualized response to medication, no single stimulant can be identified as "the best." All of the stimulants are quite similar; however, a few children will respond better to one than to any of the others. Similarly, when a troublesome side effect occurs with one of these drugs, substituting another from the same class will sometimes alleviate the problem. Cost is another, sometimes overlooked, factor. Although these medications are priced comparably, managed care organizations (HMOs) often encourage their doctors to favor the least expensive medication. Thus, many factors are involved in determining which medication is best for a particular person.

Broadly speaking, there are three ways that stimulant medications are compounded into pills: immediate release, sustained release, and a combination of both immediate and sustained release. Immediate release preparations have a fast onset of action but require multiple daily doses for effective treatment. The sustained release preparations last longer, but the onset of action is usually delayed. The preparations that combine both sustained release and long acting medication act within a few minutes after taking the pill and the effect continues from four to twelve hours, depending on the specific preparation.

Many physicians prefer to prescribe the stimulant preparations that have both a fast onset and are longer acting such as *d, l -amphetamine* (**Adderall XR**) or *methylphenidate* (**Concerta, Metadate CD**). Because the long-acting medications are usually taken once daily, doses are less likely to be skipped. Many children are teased if they take medication at school, and this can usually be avoided by using a longer acting preparation. Finally, the long-acting medications are more difficult to abuse.

How should stimulants be taken? A doctor familiar with stimulant use can determine how much and how often medication should be taken. Some children find that these medications produce mild stomach upset. To minimize this, it may be helpful to take the medicine with food. Try to be consistent; if your child takes medicine with food, try to ensure he always takes it with food. Food can change the rate as well as how much medicine is absorbed. If you change how your child takes his medicine, the size or timing of the dose may need some adjustment.

Are laboratory tests needed before or during stimulant therapy? This depends on the particular medication being used. As mentioned above, children taking *pemoline* (**Cylert**) should have frequent blood tests to measure liver function. This test should be done immediately if a child has any symptoms suggestive of liver problems. Such symptoms include persistent nausea, vomiting, abdominal pain, loss of appetite, and a change in skin color.

Children taking stimulant medications other than *pemoline* usually do not need to have routine laboratory tests done before or during drug treatment. Never-the-less, the doctor may order tests if there is any suggestion of a problem. The official FDA guidance regarding *methylphenidate* (**Concerta, Metadate, Methylin, Ritalin**, and others) states "Periodic CBC, differential, and platelet counts are advised during prolonged therapy." This is medical jargon for laboratory blood tests to examine the health of blood cells and platelets. The term "periodic" is left undefined. Since blood problems with *methylphenidate* are extremely rare, most doctors only do these tests if a child develops symptoms that might suggest a problem. Some of these symptoms might be fatigue, bruising easily, or frequent infections such as a sore throat.

What are the usual doses and available pill sizes for each of the stimulant medications? Following is a brief summary of the basic information about each of the currently available stimulant medications. The dose ranges are approximations; many children will respond best on higher or lower doses.

methylphenidate, immediate release (**Ritalin** and others). <u>Overview</u>: The most commonly prescribed medication for ADHD. The duration of action is about four hours, thus requiring multiple doses per day. <u>Available as</u>: 5 mg, 10 mg, 20 mg tablets. <u>Usual starting dose</u>: 5 mg twice daily. <u>Typical maintenance dose</u>: 15 mg in the morning, 10 mg at noon, 5 mg in the late afternoon. <u>Maximum dose</u>: 60 mg per day in divided doses.

dexmethylphenidate, immediate release (**Focalin**). <u>Overview</u>: No meaningful difference from methylphenidate other than the usual dose is exactly half that of methylphenidate. The duration of action is about four hours, thus requiring multiple doses per day. Available as: 2.5 mg, 5 mg, 10 mg tablets. Usual starting dose: 2.5 mg twice daily. Typical maintenance dose: 7.5 mg in the morning, 5 mg at noon, 2.5 mg in the late afternoon. Maximum dose: 30 mg per day in divided doses.

methylphenidate, long acting (**Metadate ER, Methylin ER, Ritalin SR,** and generics). Overview: A longer acting formulation that gradually dissolves in the digestive tract giving approximately a six-hour duration of action but with a somewhat delayed onset of action. Available as: 20 mg and 10 mg capsules. Usual starting dose: 20 mg per day. Typical maintenance dose: Most often used in combination with immediate release *methylphenidate*; for example, 20 mg SR in the morning, 10 mg immediate release at noon, 5 mg immediate release in the afternoon. Maximum dose: 60 mg per day in divided doses.

methylphenidate, immediate release and long acting (**Metadate CD**). Overview: capsules that contain 30% immediate release and 70% extended release *methylphenidate*. This combination of both sustained and immediate release may be more convenient than combining a sustained release and immediate release pill as described above. Available as: 20 mg capsules. Usual starting dose: 20 mg per day. Typical maintenance dose: 20 mg in the morning and 20 mg at noon. Maximum dose: 60 mg per day in divided doses.

methylphenidate, immediate release and long acting (**Concerta**). Overview: The **Concerta** capsule is a unique device that is designed to release *methylphenidate* in a precise fashion over a twelve-hour period. The result is that **Concerta** given once per day is comparable to immediate release *methylphenidate* given three times per day. The unique capsule also makes it nearly impossible to crush the medication into powder for purposes of abuse. **Concerta** should be used with caution in children with bowel problems or with swallowing difficulties. Because the capsule shell does not dissolve, it passes through the digestive tract unchanged. There is an extremely small possibility of a bowel obstruction in some children, particularly those with cystic fibrosis, Meckle's diverticulum, or other bowel problems. Available as: 18 mg, 36 mg, 54 mg. Usual starting dose: One 18 mg capsule per day. Typical maintenance dose: One 36 mg capsule per day. It is not usually necessary to combine with an immediate release *methylphenidate*. Maximum dose: 54 mg per day.

dextroamphetamine, immediate release (**Dexedrine**, **Dextrostat** and generics). Overview: A very common alternative to *methylphenidate*. Duration of action is about four to six hours and usually requires twice per day dosing. Available as: 5mg, 10 mg tablets. Usual starting dose: 5 mg in the morning and 5 mg at noon. Typical maintenance dose: 10 mg in the morning and 5 mg at noon. Maximum dose: 40 mg per day in divided doses.

dextroamphetamine, long acting (**Dexedrine Spansules**). Overview: A longer acting formulation that gradually dissolves in the digestive tract giving approximately an eight-hour duration of action. Twice per day dosing is still often needed, and the onset of action is somewhat delayed. Available as: 5 mg, 10 mg, 15 mg capsules. Usual starting dose: 5 mg twice daily. Typical maintenance dose: 10 mg in the morning and 10 mg in the afternoon. Maximum dose: 40 mg per day in divided doses.

d, l -amphetamine, immediate release (**Adderall**). Overview: Quite similar to the *dextroamphetamine* preparations above as it consists of 2/3 *dextroamphetamine* and 1/3 *levoamphetamine*. Some people will benefit from the presence of *levoamphetamine*; a few will experience more side effects. Available as: 5 mg, 7.5 mg, 10 mg, 12.5 mg, 15 mg, 20 mg, 30 mg tablets. Usual starting dose: 5 mg twice per day. Typical maintenance dose: 10 mg in the morning and 10 mg in the afternoon. Maximum dose: 40 mg per day in divided doses.

d, l -amphetamine, immediate release and long acting (**Adderall XR**). Overview: Capsules contain both immediate release and sustained release medication that will allow many people to be treated with once per day dosing. Available as: 10 mg, 20 mg, and 30 mg capsules. Usual starting dose: 10 mg in the morning. Typical maintenance dose: 20 mg in the morning. Maximum dose: 40 mg per day.

pemoline (**Cylert** and generics). Overview: Rarely used because of the risk for liver damage and the recommendation for blood tests every other week. It is the longest acting of the stimulants, usually given once per day. Available as: 18.75 mg, 37.5 mg, 75 mg tablets and 37.5 mg chewable tablets. Usual starting dose: 18.75 mg per day. Typical maintenance dose: 75 mg per day. Maximum dose: 112.5 mg per day.

Which side effects may occur during stimulant therapy? During the first few weeks of treatment the following side effects may appear:

Common side effects	*Rare side effects*
nervousness	confusion*
insomnia (poor sleep)	rashes*
poor appetite*	growth delay
grouchiness	seizures (extremely rare)*
stomach upset, nausea	abnormal movements*
abdominal pain	(i.e. twitches or tics)
dizziness	liver problems
headaches	(with *pemoline*)*
drowsiness	
rapid heartbeat	The asterisk (*) indicates side effects that may be serious.

Although this list may seem long, most children experience no side effects at all. When side effects do occur, they are usually mild and the child does not need to stop the medication. Some children become irritable or weepy, especially in the evening, when beginning stimulant therapy. This typically happens as the effects of the medication are wearing off and is called "behavioral rebound." If it persists or is severe, the doctor may change the dose or switch to a different medication.

Fortunately, most of these side effects are not medically dangerous. They reflect the body's initial response to stimulants, and the side effects often decrease or disappear within a few weeks. However, some side effects can persist in certain children. Those most likely to persist are upset stomach and poor appetite. Often these can be minimized by giving the medication at mealtime. Doctors routinely weigh children at follow-up appointments for ADHD; however, if your child seems to be eating much less than usual, weigh him or her weekly and bring this information to your next appointment.

Informing the doctor about side effects is important. Most need not be mentioned until the next scheduled appointment. However, if any are particularly distressing, are troubling to the child, or are interfering with the child's day-to-day activities, it is prudent to contact the doctor sooner.

Are there delayed side effects from stimulants? Some stimulant side effects can occur weeks to months after treatment has started. These include mood instability and slowing of growth.

> *Mood instability.* Many children taking stimulants experience a mild instability in their mood. This typically occurs in the late afternoon or evening as the effects of the last dose of medication taken that day wear off. Parents often comment that their child seems "grouchy" or "difficult" toward the end of the day. Occasionally, such mood instability can become severe enough to warrant changing to a different medication. This problem most often occurs with the short acting stimulant preparations.

> *Slowing of growth.* For reasons that are not clear, a few children grow more slowly, both in height and weight, while receiving stimulant therapy. When this occurs, the degree of growth suppression is typically mild. Slowed growth may be linked to the suppression of appetite that can occur with stimulant treatment. Because of this possibility, it is important to ensure that children on stimulant therapy receive tasty, well-balanced meals. In addition, some children do not need to take medication during holidays and summer vacations. Their growth will often "catch up" during these periods off treatment. Fortunately, prolonged growth suppression is an uncommon side effect. On very rare occasions appetite or growth problems are severe and persistent and an alternative medication should be considered.

Are there stimulant side effects for which a doctor should be contacted immediately? Yes! These include abnormal body movements, confusion, seizures, and rashes. Each is discussed below.

> *Abnormal body movements.* Some children with ADHD appear predisposed to tic disorders including Tourette's disorder. Tics are characterized by involuntary muscle movements such as eye blinking, shoulder shrugging, lip pursing, and others. Children can also have vocal tics. For example, they may grunt, repeatedly clear their throats, or swear for no apparent reason. Tourette's disorder is diagnosed when children have both vocal tics and tics involving movement. Rarely, symptoms of Tourette's disorder have appeared just after stimulant therapy was started. In some of these children, the Tourette's disorder remained when the stimulant was discontinued, although tics usually disappear when a stimulant is discontinued. If

any abnormal muscle movements or vocal tics appear, the physician should be notified immediately. In most cases it is not known whether stimulant treatment occasionally induces Tourette's disorder, or whether stimulant treatment makes a pre-existing Tourette's disorder emerge in a more visible form.

Confusion. On rare occasions children become confused or disoriented when taking stimulants. If a child shows signs of confusion or becomes extremely irritable or very withdrawn, the stimulant should be stopped and the doctor should be contacted promptly.

Seizures. Although extremely rare, a child treated with stimulants may experience a seizure. If this occurs, take the child to an emergency room without delay.

Allergic reactions. Some children, particularly those with other allergies, may be allergic to a particular stimulant preparation. If a child develops a rash, stop the medication and call the doctor as soon as possible. Occasionally allergic reactions may be severe enough to cause wheezing, swelling of the hands or face, or an extremely itchy rash. Should any of these occur, contact a doctor immediately or go to an emergency room.

These serious side effects are extremely rare and probably occur no more frequently with stimulant medications than with many over-the-counter medications. However, if they do occur, prompt action may help prevent serious injury.

What are signs and symptoms of a stimulant overdose? A variety of symptoms can result from a stimulant overdose and may include vomiting, agitation, tremors, muscle twitching, convulsions (seizures), confusion, hallucinations, sweating, flushing, headache, fever, and high blood pressure. Stimulant overdose is a serious medical emergency and if suspected, a physician should be contacted immediately. Stimulant overdose sometimes occurs when a younger sibling, imitating a brother or sister, swallows the medication intended for the older sibling. All medications must be kept away from small children. Adults should never tell children that a medicine is candy to persuade them to take it.

Tricyclic antidepressants (TCAs)

While stimulants are usually the best medication choice for ADHD, some children cannot take them because of side effects. Other children simply do not obtain adequate benefit from the various stimulants. In these instances, an alternative medication should be considered. In this section, we discuss one such alternative, the tricyclic antidepressants, commonly abbreviated as "TCAs."

There are currently nine TCAs available in the U.S. as listed in Table II (page 31). Although they differ slightly from one another, they have much in common. Because of this, they will be discussed as a group unless otherwise noted.

TCA medications have been used in psychiatry for more than 30 years as effective treatments for depression in adults. When treating depressed children in the past, a few doctors noticed that symptoms of ADHD seemed to improve as well. This eventually led to clinical studies that clearly showed one TCA, *desipramine* (**Norpramin**), was an effective treatment for many people with ADHD. Other TCAs such as *nortriptyline* (**Pamelor**) and *imipramine* (**Tofranil**) are also effective but have not been as extensively studied as *desipramine*.

What are the beneficial effects of TCAs? Like stimulants, TCAs increase attention span and decrease hyperactivity. However, TCAs are generally not quite as effective as stimulants for ADHD. This is one reason why they are considered to be "second line" treatments for ADHD. TCAs also have mood elevating properties, can improve certain sleep problems, and can be helpful for anxiety (nervousness or worry). Such features set them apart from stimulants and are often beneficial to children whose ADHD is accompanied by these difficulties.

What are the differences among TCAs? TCAs are all very closely related compounds. It is believed that there is little difference among them regarding their effectiveness for treating ADHD. Despite many similarities, there are some important differences among the various TCAs. *Amitriptyline* (**Elavil**), *amoxapine* (**Asendin**), *clomipramine* (**Anafranil**), *imipramine* (**Tofranil**), and *trimipramine* (**Surmontil**) tend to be sedating (cause sleepiness) while the rest of the TCAs appear to be substantially less sedating and may even produce a feeling of increased alertness. *Clomipramine* appears to be the most effective TCA for treating anxiety, although *amitriptyline* and *imipramine* can also be helpful to lesser degrees.

There are also important differences in the side effects of TCAs. These are discussed on the following page.

Table II: Tricyclic Antidepressants

Brand Name	Generic Name
Elavil	amitriptyline
Asendin	amoxapine
Anafranil	clomipramine
Norpramin	desipramine
Adapin, Sinequan	doxepin
Tofranil	imipramine
Aventyl	nortriptyline
Vivactil	protriptyline
Surmontil	trimipramine

Which TCA is best for ADHD? *Desipramine* is the TCA most extensively studied for the treatment of ADHD. This does not necessarily mean that it is better than the other TCAs. Over the past several years many physicians have come to prefer *nortriptyline* because it may affect the heart less than other TCAs. In situations where anxiety is a significant factor, *amitriptyline*, *clomipramine*, or *imipramine* may be preferred.

How should TCAs be taken? A doctor familiar with the use of TCAs in children is best able to determine how much medication should be taken and how often. Some children find that the medication produces a mild stomach upset. Taking it with food may minimize this. When used for ADHD, TCA medications are usually taken once a day in the morning, but sometimes doses are divided into several smaller ones over the span of a day. Never increase a child's TCA dose without first consulting the physician.

What is the usual dose of a TCA?   The effective dose of a TCA varies greatly from child to child. This is because there is great variation in the speed at which different children metabolize these medications. Because of this, making a generalization about the usual dose is meaningless.

Do TCAs have side effects?   Yes! One of the drawbacks of TCA treatment is the potential for side effects. Most children taking them will, at times, experience a few minor side effects. Sometimes, however, distressing side effects occur, and an alternative medication will need to be considered.

Below is a listing of common, as well as rare, TCA side effects. It is important to note that some of the TCAs are more likely to produce certain types of side effects than others. For example, *imipramine* is more likely than *desipramine* to produce sleepiness, and *desipramine* probably causes rashes more often than *nortriptyline*. Therefore, if one of the TCAs is helping the ADHD but has led to one or two minor but annoying side effects, it is often useful to consider an alternative TCA.

Common side effects	*Rare side effects*
agitation	heart rhythm changes*
blurred vision	high blood pressure*
constipation*	psychosis/mania*
diarrhea	rapid heart-rate
dry mouth and eyes	seizures*
restlessness	difficulty urinating*
sleepiness	The asterisk (*) indicates side
weight gain	effects that may be serious.

Which side effects occur early in TCA therapy?   When children first begin taking TCAs, minor side effects may occur as their bodies adjust to the medication. Many of these early side effects diminish gradually during the first few weeks of treatment. For example, early in treatment children commonly notice a slightly dry mouth, mild constipation, and some daytime sleepiness. If side effects like these are not causing great discomfort, it is usually best to wait a few weeks to see if they subside on their own. If unpleasant side effects continue for more than two weeks, this should be discussed with the child's doctor.

Are there side effects from TCAs that may not occur right away? Yes. Although it is more common for side effects to appear early in treatment and then diminish gradually, on occasion side effects appear late in treatment. Some examples include a gradual, yet persistent weight gain, worsening constipation, and liver problems. It is always wise to consult the child's physician if any late emerging side effects appear.

Are there TCA-related side effects for which a doctor should be contacted immediately? Yes! TCAs occasionally cause changes in a child's heart rhythm. This may be experienced as shortness of breath, fainting or "passing out," dizziness, chest pain, or a sensation of a "pounding" heart. If the child experiences any of these problems, they should be reported to the child's doctor as soon as possible. Many times these symptoms are *not* related to changes in heart rhythm. For example, TCAs also can cause low blood pressure, especially when standing up quickly. Symptoms of low blood pressure may also include fainting, dizziness, weakness, or a pounding heart. Whatever the cause of these symptoms, your child's physician may wish to obtain an electrocardiogram (abbreviated as either EKG or ECG) and certain blood tests to better understand the problem. The EKG is a simple and painless test that measures the electrical activity of the heart.

Difficulty urinating can be a serious side effect of TCAs. While taking TCAs, a few boys may notice that their urinary stream is less powerful and that there is some difficulty or hesitancy in starting the flow of urine. Because of anatomical differences, this almost never happens to girls. When mild, this side effect is of little consequence. On very rare occasion, however, some boys find that they cannot urinate at all. As the bladder fills, it becomes very uncomfortable making it all the more difficult for him to relax enough to urinate. This can happen quite unpredictably, even to a boy who has taken a TCA for some time without trouble. It also may result from an increase in dose, or the addition of another medication. Obviously, a child with this problem should be taken to an emergency room soon, as his discomfort will only increase.

Are laboratory tests necessary during TCA treatment? In most cases, yes. TCAs can sometimes affect body organs including the heart and liver. Because of this, many physicians recommend obtaining an EKG and certain blood tests during TCA treatment. Because these problems are quite rare, other physicians do not routinely obtain these tests for children who are perfectly healthy and not experiencing side effects from the TCA.

What are signs and symptoms of a TCA overdose? An overdose of a TCA is *always* a medical emergency. A typical early sign of overdose is a change in the child's mental state. This can appear as extreme sleepiness, confusion, or agitation. Later on, the child may become unconscious, develop seizures, or even have a cardiac arrest. If a TCA overdose is even suspected, the child should be transported immediately to an emergency room, preferably by ambulance.

Bupropion (Wellbutrin, Zyban)

Bupropion (**Wellbutrin**) is a unique antidepressant that is chemically very different from other antidepressants. The medication itself has stimulant-like effects. The *bupropion* molecule is modified in the patient's liver during metabolism, changing it to a compound that has antidepressant effects. Thus, *bupropion* is like two medications in one!

What are the beneficial effects of *bupropion* (**Wellbutrin**)? Like the stimulant medications, *bupropion* increases attention span and decreases hyperactivity. In a recent study of children with ADHD, *bupropion* appeared to be nearly as effective as modest doses of a stimulant. In addition, *bupropion* has antidepressant properties, making it a very useful medication for children with both ADHD and mood symptoms. It is also an effective aid to control nicotine-withdrawal symptoms when stopping smoking. When used as a smoking-cessation aid, *bupropion* is marketed under the brand name **Zyban**.

What is the correct dose of *bupropion* (**Wellbutrin**)? There are presently two formulations of *bupropion,* standard and sustained-release (**Wellbutrin SR**). The total daily dose should not exceed 450 mg of the standard preparation, or 400 mg of the sustained-release. These guidelines are for adults. In the case of children, especially small children, your child's doctor may adjust these guidelines accordingly. Usually, 225 to 300 mg per day, in divided doses, is adequate to control ADHD symptoms. As with other medications, the correct dose of *bupropion* must be individualized.

How should *bupropion* (**Wellbutrin**) **be taken?** It is best to discuss this with a physician familiar with prescribing *bupropion* to children. Most often, the standard preparation is prescribed in three doses over the course of the day, while the sustained-release preparation is typically taken once or twice per day.

Does *bupropion* (**Wellbutrin**) **have side effects?** Like all medications, *bupropion* may cause side effects. Often these side effects are temporary and occur early in treatment. Although the list below may seem long, many children experience no side effects from *bupropion* at the doses used for ADHD, and tolerate it without difficulty. On rare occasions the use of *bupropion* has led to seizures. Because of this, the drug should not be taken in high doses, or by individuals with a seizure disorder.

Seizures have also occurred in patients taking *bupropion* who have eating disorders, such as anorexia nervosa and bulimia. Anorexia nervosa is a disorder in which patients greatly restrict their food intake and bulimia is a disorder in which patients deliberately (usually secretly) vomit after a meal. It is unclear exactly why this increases the risk of a *bupropion*-related seizure, but children with an eating disorder should not take *bupropion*.

Common side effects	*Rare side effects*
rash*	blood pressure changes*
dizziness	seizure*
constipation*	
confusion	
dry mouth	
fatigue	The asterisk (*) indicates side effects that may be serious.
headache	
excessive sweating	
nausea	
nervousness/agitation	
tremor	
weight loss*	

Which side effects occur early in *bupropion* **(Wellbutrin) therapy?**
Many times *bupropion* does not cause any side effects. However, a few children will experience stomach upset or headache when starting this drug. Because these are such common occurrences, it is difficult to tell whether they are related to the medication. When one of these minor problems occurs, it is best to tell the doctor about it at the child's next appointment. Sometimes early in *bupropion* treatment, a rash will appear. If this happens, it is best to contact the doctor promptly for further instructions.

Are there *bupropion* **(Wellbutrin) side effects that may not occur right away?** Side effects which appear late in treatment are quite uncommon with *bupropion*. Usually, if side effects are going to be a problem, they occur early in treatment. One exception is when the dose of *bupropion* is raised. Sometimes this results in the occurrence of side effects that did not occur at the lower dose. For example, an increase in *bupropion* dose may result in difficulty falling asleep, or produce a sensation of nervousness or "jitteriness".

Are there *bupropion* **(Wellbutrin) side effects for which a doctor should be contacted immediately?** Yes! Very rarely *bupropion* can cause a seizure. Normally this occurs only when children are taking relatively high doses. Because of this small but serious risk, *bupropion* is usually not prescribed in amounts greater than 450 mg per day for the standard preparation and 400 mg per day for the sustained-release preparation. In addition, no single dose of the standard preparation should exceed 150 mg. When the sustained-release preparation is used, single doses up to 200 mg are usually permissible; although in the case of a small child, the maximum safe dose will be less. Many physicians prefer the sustained release form of the medication because it may have a somewhat smaller risk of causing seizures. If a seizure occurs, the child should be taken to the nearest emergency room without delay.

Are laboratory tests necessary during *bupropion* **(Wellbutrin) treatment?** Laboratory tests are not usually necessary during treatment with *bupropion*. While this is a general rule, on some occasions, certain laboratory tests may be performed if a child is taking any additional medications, has a pre-existing medical problem, or develops a medical problem while taking *bupropion*.

What are signs and symptoms of a *bupropion* **(Wellbutrin) overdose?** The signs and symptoms of a *bupropion* overdose may not be immediately apparent. Depending on the size of the overdose, there may be few if any symptoms. However, children usually experience nervousness, upset stomach, or headache. In large overdoses, children may become confused or disoriented. Because seizures are common with a *bupropion* overdose, it is very important to bring the child to an emergency room immediately if an overdose is suspected.

Clonidine (Catapres) and *guanfacine* (Tenex)

Clonidine (**Catapres**) and *guanfacine* (**Tenex**) are two very similar medications that were originally developed to treat high blood pressure. Because each of these medications affect the brain chemicals known as adrenergic neurotransmitters, researchers hypothesized that they would be helpful in treating ADHD. Several subsequent studies have confirmed that these medications do help some children with ADHD.

What are the beneficial effects of *clonidine* (**Catapres**) **and** *guanfacine* (**Tenex**)? Both medications can help reduce hyperactivity and improve attention span in some children with ADHD. Because these medications can cause drowsiness, they may also benefit children who have trouble falling asleep.

How is *clonidine* (**Catapres**) **or** *guanfacine* (**Tenex**) **therapy started?** Both *clonidine* and *guanfacine* can produce sedation (sleepiness) early in treatment. To minimize this, a small dose is prescribed initially, then gradually increased over several weeks. On rare occasions, these medications affect heart rhythm so some physicians will obtain an EKG before prescribing. The EKG is a simple, painless test that measures the electrical activity of the heart. It is sometimes used as a precautionary measure to detect any preexisting heart problems that could be aggravated by *clonidine* or *guanfacine* treatment.

What are the correct doses of *clonidine* (**Catapres**) **and** *guanfacine* (**Tenex**)? The best dose is usually the minimum amount that produces a satisfactory result. This can vary considerably from child to child and is best determined by a physician familiar with treating ADHD. *Clonidine* is usually taken three times per day with each dose typically being 0.1 mg. *Guanfacine* is also taken three times per day with each dose being approximately 1.0 mg.

How should *clonidine* (**Catapres**) **or** *guanfacine* (**Tenex**) **be taken?** This is best determined by a doctor familiar with prescribing these medications for children. It is usually most convenient to take *clonidine* at mealtimes since this drug is almost always taken three or more times per day, and meals can serve as a reminder. Sometimes *guanfacine* is an effective ADHD treatment with once or twice daily dosing.

Are any laboratory tests necessary during *clonidine* (**Catapres**) **or** *guanfacine* (**Tenex**) **treatment?** Laboratory tests usually are not needed. However, the doctor may request an EKG from time to time to ensure that the heart is functioning normally. This is especially important for those experiencing side effects such as shortness of breath, palpitations, or chest pain. Obtaining an EKG is also advisable if the child plans to participate in competitive, highly strenuous athletic activities. Most physicians also routinely check the child's blood pressure from time to time.

Which side effects occur early in c*lonidine* (**Catapres**) **or** *guanfacine* (**Tenex**) **therapy?** As mentioned previously, almost every child who begins treatment with either of these medications experiences some sleepiness. Over a few weeks, this side effect gradually disappears for most children. However, a few children are unusually sensitive to this side effect and if it remains a problem, it may be necessary to reduce the dose or consider an alternative medication.

Another side effect some children experience while taking these medications is low blood pressure. Symptoms include tiredness and dizziness. The child may even look somewhat pale and listless. If these symptoms occur, the doctor should be informed. Other side effects are listed below.

Common side effects	*Rare side effects*
constipation*	low blood pressure*
rash	heart rhythm changes*
headache	depression*
weight gain	
dizziness	The asterisk (*) indicates side
high blood pressure*	effects that may be serious.
(if drug is withdrawn too quickly)	

Are there c*lonidine* (**Catapres**) **or** *guanfacine* (**Tenex**) **side effects that might not occur right away?** When side effects occur, most appear early in treatment, but a few can occur later. For example, some children taking *clonidine* or *guanfacine* gain a substantial amount of weight. Often, however, the medication is only one reason for weight gain; lack of exercise, overeating, and a genetic predisposition are often additional contributing factors. When weight gain becomes a problem, the first step is to help the child adopt a healthy lifestyle that includes a sensible diet and regular vigorous exercise. Another uncommon side effect that can develop over time is depression. Some children taking these medications will experience a gradual deterioration in mood. They may become irritable, sad, or have low energy. These symptoms of depression can "creep up" slowly and may not be noticed until the child is in significant distress. If your child's mood takes a downturn, discuss this with the doctor.

Do clonidine (**Catapres**) **or** guanfacine (**Tenex**) **have any serious side effects?** Although extremely rare, a few children experience dangerously low blood pressure when treated with clonidine or guanfacine. This is quite apparent because they will be extremely weak and may be unable to stand up. Sometimes problems with low blood pressure seem to come and go. Children may feel fine most of the time, but when they stand up, take a hot shower, or are overheated they may feel very lightheaded, dizzy, weak, and nauseated. Another extremely rare side effect is an abnormal heart rhythm. This can be experienced as a pounding sensation in the chest, fainting, or shortness of breath. If any of these symptoms occur, the child's doctor should be contacted as soon as possible.

How should clonidine (**Catapres**) **or** guanfacine (**Tenex**) **treatment be stopped?** The dose should gradually be reduced before being stopped completely. If these medications are stopped too quickly, children may experience a sudden increase in their blood pressure. This is called "rebound hypertension." Although this is typically mild, it can sometimes be high enough to cause a severe headache or possibly a stroke. Therefore, it is wise to taper the medication slowly while checking the child's blood pressure daily. The blood pressure should also be checked daily during the week *after* the medication has been completely stopped. This precaution is an inconvenience, but a recent research report has shown that rebound hypertension may be more common than previously realized. It is especially important if the child has been on the medication a long time or at a high dose. Schools nurses may be willing to check the child's blood pressure and many pharmacies and fire stations will also check blood pressure at no cost. The doctor's office may also be willing to perform this service.

What are signs and symptoms of a *clonidine* (**Catapres**) **or** *guanfacine* (**Tenex**) **overdose?** A *clonidine* or *guanfacine* overdose is a serious medical emergency, and the child should be brought to the emergency room immediately. The most obvious symptom is extreme sleepiness; the child may even be comatose and, if left untreated, could stop breathing or experience a cardiac arrest.

Additional commonly asked questions

What should be done if a child skips a dose of medication? This is a common occurrence and is usually not cause for alarm. For medications that are given twice or more per day, the child should not take the missed dose late if more than two hours have passed, nor increase subsequent doses to "make up" for the missed dose. If one dose has been missed, the child should take the next dose at the next prescribed time. For medications that are taken once per day, the missed dose can usually be taken up to four hours late without causing a problem. If several doses have been missed, or if you are uncertain, it is advisable to contact the child's doctor for advice on how to proceed.

What should be done if a dose of medication is mistakenly taken twice? These medications have enough of a safety margin that this is not usually dangerous. It is, however, likely that your child will feel uncomfortable. Depending on the specific medication, he may feel sleepy, jittery, or dizzy. In the case of teens, they should not drive a car until the next day and even then, only if they feel recovered. However, when this happens, you should still *always* contact your child's doctor (or the person on call for your doctor) for further advice. A few children may need medical treatment in this situation—especially if they have a medical condition or if they are taking several medications.

Do ADHD medications interact with other prescription medications? Sometimes. It would be impossible to list all of the potential interactions between ADHD medications and other drugs. It is recommended that children taking ADHD medications not be given other medication without first consulting the doctor or checking with a pharmacist. If a child has more than one doctor, it is important that all of them are kept informed of all the medications your child is taking. This will help reduce the possibility of one of the doctors prescribing a medication that could lead to a medication interaction.

Do ADHD medications interact with over-the-counter medicines, such as cough syrups or cold remedies? Occasionally over-the-counter medications can interact with ADHD medications producing unexpected results. Taking them along with an ADHD medication is not a good idea. It is best to always consult with your child's doctor or pharmacist before any other drugs are given, including over-the-counter products. One exception is that an occasional dose of acetaminophen (Tylenol) is almost always OK.

Can a child become addicted to stimulants? The term *addiction* implies that the individual craves the drug and will go to extraordinary lengths to obtain it. This almost never occurs in children who are being treated with stimulants for ADHD, especially when these medications are being taken as prescribed. Children who have taken stimulant medications for long periods of time may have withdrawal symptoms if the medication is stopped abruptly. These symptoms may include any of the following: sleepiness, grogginess, depression, lack of ambition, and irritability. Because of potential withdrawal symptoms, stimulant medications should be discontinued gradually whenever possible.

Problems of addiction with these medications usually occur when doses are increased without the advice of a doctor. Occasionally, adults or adolescents have abused stimulants by taking large doses to "get high" or by selling them on the street. Since stimulants have been abused, they are now carefully regulated. Physicians and pharmacists keep careful records of the amount of stimulant medication given and may express concern if prescriptions are lost or if there are requests for renewals more frequently than prescribed.

Frequently articles appear in the popular press that decry the use of stimulants to treat ADHD and label these medications as "dangerous, highly addictive, harsh chemicals." Over-dramatization sells magazines, but it is irresponsible and does a disservice to those children who struggle with the disorder. Ethical journalists never write such articles.

It is true that many teenagers experiment with stimulant abuse by obtaining medication from friends being treated for ADHD. This is very similar to the experimentation that is done with alcohol and tobacco. Unlike alcohol and tobacco, however, experimentation with stimulants almost never leads to continued long-term use.

Can a child become addicted to the other medications (besides stimulants) used to treat ADHD? None of the other medications used to treat ADHD are addictive. They simply do not produce anything remotely resembling a "high." Even so, some misguided individuals will attempt to abuse them. They may "snort" them (inhale powdered medication up the nose) or smoke them by placing ground up medication in a cigarette or pipe. Such practices can be dangerous and may produce serious unexpected adverse effects.

Can a child grow up to become a drug abuser because of stimulant treatment now? Long-term follow-up studies have clearly shown that treating ADHD children with stimulants does *not* increase their risk for drug addiction. Instead, stimulant treatment dramatically *reduces* the risk of substance abuse problems. This is a very pronounced effect, making it an important factor to consider when weighing the advantages and disadvantages of stimulant medication treatment.

Do stimulants or other medications for ADHD ever stop working in a child? Occasionally, stimulants seem to lose their effectiveness after a period of time. This is known as "tolerance" and when it develops, an increase in dose or change to another medication is often helpful. Another approach is to stop the medication for awhile and then resume it at a later date. This is not always practical because it means that the child will be left untreated for a period of time.

Sometimes when stimulants seem to have stopped working, it is actually because the child has developed new problems. For example, if a child develops a mood disorder (such as depression), this will reduce his ability to concentrate. Similarly, if new family stresses such as divorce or medical illness occur, this too can adversely affect a child, giving the appearance that the medication is no longer working.

Shouldn't children and parents learn to overcome difficulties without drugs? Of course! Stimulant medications are not a cure-all for poor parenting skills, a chaotic family life, or chronic discipline problems. However, ADHD is a disorder, not a simple problem of life. Just as no one expects a child to cope with problems such as pneumonia or diabetes without medication, neither should children be expected to grapple with ADHD without medications.

Aren't stimulants over-prescribed? There is evidence to suggest that some physicians prescribe stimulants without a careful diagnostic evaluation. Even though stimulant medications can make children who do not have ADHD easier to manage, this is not an appropriate use for them. If parents or teachers are having difficulty managing a *normally energetic youngster*, there are better alternatives to medication. These include parent training classes to enhance skills, or providing the teacher with a more manageable class size or a classroom aide.

Ensuring that each child being assessed has a complete evaluation by a physician familiar with ADHD and stimulant therapy can help to avoid over-prescribing. Following this evaluation, a frank discussion between the doctor, parents, and child (when appropriate) about the various treatment options, including medications, will lead to the most appropriate treatment.

Can the long-term use of stimulants or other ADHD medications harm a child? Stimulants have been used for the treatment of ADHD for more than 40 years. Long-term studies examining this question give no evidence to suggest that the long-term use of stimulants causes harm. As mentioned elsewhere in this booklet, a few studies have suggested that some children may have their growth slowed if stimulants are taken continuously for a long time. However, other studies suggest that growth ultimately "catches up" in adolescence (see also page 28), particularly if treatment is no longer needed. It is unclear whether this occurs in those who need stimulant treatment throughout childhood and adolescence, although the available data suggest that the ultimate impact on height is very small (on the order of an inch or less). Thus, the long-term use of stimulants, prescribed in appropriate doses for ADHD, appears safe.

It has been shown that high doses of *methylphenidate* can cause cancer in laboratory animals. While this finding is certainly cause for concern and further research, increased rates of cancer have not been seen in humans. Several researchers are continuing to gather data in an effort to answer this question with more certainty.

If a child has severe ADHD, can several medications be used together? Occasionally, medication combinations such as a stimulant combined with an antidepressant can be beneficial. However, this should never be done unless treatment with a single agent has been tried first. Presently there is little research on combining psychiatric medications in children, and doing so increases the risk of side effects considerably. If a drug combination is under consideration, it is best to obtain a consultation (or second opinion) with a physician highly familiar with ADHD and the use of psychiatric medications in children.

Can ADHD be treated with caffeine? Probably not, although there is some research that suggests that caffeine may exert a mildly beneficial effect. However, at reasonable caffeine doses this effect is too small to benefit the child. At high doses, caffeine produces objectionable side effects such as nervousness and sweating. Furthermore, the effects of caffeine seem to be less predictable than the effects of prescribed stimulant medications.

Can a child taking a medication for ADHD participate in sports?
Experience has shown that children taking stimulant medication can participate in athletic activities without any special restrictions. Still, some caution is advised for children taking non-stimulant medications or medication combinations. Extremely strenuous and exhausting activities such as marathon races, or competitive activities such as soccer or basketball games, can lead to overheating or dehydration. When this happens, the non-stimulant medications (TCAs, as well as *clonidine* and *guanfacine*) can produce side effects that would not occur under normal circumstances, including disturbances in the heart rhythm, fainting, seizure, or very high body temperature (heat stroke).

We recommend that children taking non-stimulant medications avoid participating in sports if the weather is very hot, and that they be encouraged to stop and rest if they begin to feel ill. Adult supervision of sport activities is also very important. Competition can sometimes lead to children pushing themselves to the point of exhaustion, despite being warned about overexertion. Coaches and other supervising adults need to be aware that a child is on a medication that could lead to difficulties if the child becomes exhausted.

Of course, all children who plan to participate in extremely vigorous sport activities, whether or not they are receiving ADHD medication, should undergo a physical examination by a physician before participating.

Some sports organizations require drug testing of participants and a positive test for stimulants may be grounds for disqualification. Athletes should investigate the rules for their sport prior to competition. In some cases, a letter from the treating physician is all that is needed. In other cases, stimulants are absolutely forbidden.

What is the youngest age that a child can be treated with medication?
There is no exact "cutoff" age at which a child is too young to be treated. It is uncommon to treat children before kindergarten-age because ADHD usually causes little impairment in very young children. However, a few young children with severe ADHD are so hyperactive and impulsive that they are unable to develop normal social skills. Such children may be impossible to keep in a day-care setting and can be so difficult to care for that their parents' ability to cope is stretched to the limit. In these cases, medication treatment is a reasonable consideration. Unfortunately, medication response and side effects are less predictable in very young children. Because of these issues, it is best to consult with a specialist (such as a child psychiatrist or a child neurologist) who is experienced and knowledgeable in treating psychiatric disorders in the very young.

Do children outgrow ADHD? The answer is a definite "sometimes." Most children experience a decrease in their ADHD symptoms around the time of puberty and sometimes earlier. Some of these children can then discontinue ADHD medication therapy and function quite well. However, a percentage of children with ADHD will continue to have problems through their teen years and even on into adulthood. These individuals may need medication treatment for a much greater period of time.

As children grow and develop, their medication treatment should be periodically re-assessed. For example, as they grow larger a bigger dose of medication may be needed. On the other hand, if their symptoms diminish, a smaller dose of medication may be adequate. In a few cases, a different medication may be needed because of physiological changes that occur in children as they develop.

Do adults suffer ADHD? Yes! At one time it was thought that ADHD was only a disorder of childhood. However, over the past 15 years it has been "discovered" that this disorder can persist into adulthood and those who continue to have symptoms can benefit from treatment. Adults with ADHD have many of the same symptoms as children except that adults tend to show less physical overactivity. As with children, the decision to treat ADHD in adults is a complex one that must take many factors into consideration.

Because adult ADHD is a recently recognized phenomenon, it may be difficult to find physicians experienced in treating this disorder. It may be necessary to contact a large medical center or a university medical school for treatment. For more information, see *ADHD in Adults: A Guide* (see page 52 for ordering information).

How can someone learn all that is important about ADHD and its treatment? Obviously, a booklet of this size cannot provide answers to every question about childhood ADHD. The material included here was selected because doctors and parents of children suffering from ADHD felt it was especially important.

The following suggestions may help you learn more about ADHD:

- Read this booklet thoroughly, making sure to note any areas where you have questions.

- Ask your doctor these questions and any others you have.

- Re-read the booklet from time to time to refresh your memory.

- Share it with family members and close friends and discuss the areas that are of particular importance to you.

- Refer to the readings suggested on the following pages. Non-technical items can often be obtained through a local public library or bookstore. Technical items can usually be obtained from a university medical library.

- Self-help groups have formed in many different parts of the country. These groups offer support and information to families with children who have ADHD. Your doctor or a school psychologist may have information about support groups near you.

- A national non-profit organization called CHADD (Children and Adults With Attention Deficit Disorders) can provide further information and a referral to a local chapter in your area. Contact: CHADD, 8181 Professional Place, Suite 201, Landover, MD 20785.
  Phone (800) 233-4050. Fax(301) 306-7090.
  E-mail: national@chadd.org. Web site: www.chadd.org.

- The National Attention Deficit Disorder Association (National ADDA) also provides information and is more specifically focused on ADHD in adults. Contact: National ADDA, 1788 Second Street, Suite 200, Highland Park, IL 60035. Phone: (847) 432-2332 (to leave a message). Fax: (847) 432-5874. E-Mail: mail@add.org. Web site: www.add.org.

- ADDvance is an organization devoted to ADHD in women and girls. Contact: ADDvance Magazine, 1001 Spring Street, Suite 206, Silver Spring, MD 20910. Phone (888) 238-8588. Fax (301) 562-8449.
  E-mail: editors@addvance.com. Web site: www.addvance.com.

Suggested Readings

Non-technical

ADD/ADHD Behavior-Change Resource Kit: Ready-To-Use Strategies & Activities for Helping Children With Attention Deficit Disorder. Flick GL. Center for Applied Research in Education, Des Moines, IA, 1998

ADHD: A Teenagers Guide. Crist JJ. Childswork/Childsplay, Plainview, NY, 1996

All About Attention Deficit Disorder. Phelan TW. Child Management, Inc., Glenellyn, IL, 2nd ed., 2000

Answers to Distraction. Hallowell EM, Ratey JJ. Bantam Books, New York, 1996

The Attention Deficit Answer Book: The Best Medications and Parenting Strategies for Your Child. Wachtel A, Boyette M. Dutton/Plume, New York, 1998

Attention-Deficit/Hyperactivity Disorder: What Every Parent Wants to Know. Wodrich DL. Paul H. Brookes Publishing Co., Towson, MD, rev. ed., 1999

Attention, Please! A Comprehensive Guide for Successfully Parenting Children with Attention Disorders and Hyperactivity (ADHD/ADD). Copeland ED, Love VL. Specialty Pr. Inc., Plantation, FL, rev. ed., 1996

Dr. Larry Silver's Advice to Parents on Attention Deficit Hyperactivity Disorder. Silver LB. Time Books, New York, Paperback copy, 1999

Driven to Distraction: Recognizing and Coping With Attention Deficit Disorder From Childhood Through Adulthood. Hallowell EM, Ratey JJ. Simon & Schuster, New York, Paperback copy, 1995

Fathering the ADHD Child: A Book for Fathers, Mothers, and Professionals. Jacobs EH. Jason Aaron, Northvale, NJ, 1998

Help4ADD@High School. Nadeau K. Advantage Books, Bethesda, MD, 1998

Is it "Just a Phase?" How to Tell Common Childhood Phases From More Serious Problems. Swedo SA, Leonard HL. Broadway, New York, Paperback copy, 1999

Learning to Slow Down and Pay Attention: A Book for Kids About ADD. Nadeau KG, Dixon EB. Magination Press, New York, 1997

Pay Attention, Slosh. Smith M. Albert Whitman & Co., Morton Grove, IL, 1997

Power Parenting for Children with ADD/ADHD: A Practical Parent's Guide for Managing Difficult Behaviors. Flick GL. Center for Applied Research in Education, West Nyack, NY, 1996

Straight Talk about Psychiatric Medications for Kids. Wilens TE, Guilford Press, New York, Paperback copy, 1998

Taking Charge of ADHD: The Complete, Authoritative Guide for Parents. Barkley, RA. Guilford Press, New York, rev. ed., 2000

Teenagers with ADD: A Parents' Guide (The Special-Needs Collection). Dendy CAZ. Woodbine House, Bethesda, MD, 1995

Voices From Fatherhood: Fathers, Sons, and ADHD. Kilcarr PJ. Quinn PO, Brunner/Mazel Trade, Bristol, PA, 1997

Technical

All About ADHD: The Complete Practical Guide For Classroom Teachers. Pfiffner LJ. Scholastic Trade, Jefferson City, MO, 1999

Attention Deficit Disorder: Practical Coping Methods. Fisher BC, Beckley RA. CRC Press, Boca Raton, FL, 1998

Attention Deficit Disorders and Comorbidities in Children, Adolescents, and Adults. Brown TE, ed. American Psychiatric Press, Washington, D.C., 2000

Attention-Deficit Hyperactivity Disorder: A Handbook for Diagnosis and Treatment. Barkley RA. Guilford Press, New York, 2nd ed., 1998

Attention-Deficit/Hyperactivity Disorder: A Clinical Guide to Diagnosis and Treatment for Health and Mental Health Professionals. Silver LB. American Psychiatric Press, Washington, D.C., 2nd ed., 1999

Attention Deficit Hyperactivity Disorder (In Adults and Children): The Latest Assessment and Treatment Strategies. Conners CK, Jett J. Compact Clinicals, Kansas City, MO, 1999

A Comprehensive Guide To Attention Deficit Disorder In Adults: Research, Diagnosis, and Treatment. Nadeau K (ed.). Brunner/Mazel, New York, 1995

Managing Attention and Learning Disorders in Late Adolescence and Adulthood: A Guide for Practitioners. Goldstein S, et al. John Wiley & Sons, New York, 1997

Ordering Information

We hope to revise and update this booklet from time to time. Your comments, suggestions, and criticisms are most welcome. To share your ideas or order additional copies of this guidebook, please contact:

Information Centers
Madison Institute of Medicine, Inc.
7617 Mineral Point Rd, Suite 300
Madison, WI 53717 USA
Telephone (608) 827-2470
Fax (608) 827-2479
E-mail: mim@miminc.org

The Madison Institute of Medicine is a not-for-profit organization. Its Information Centers are dependent, in part, on user fees and contributions for support.

PRICES (Subject to change)	
1-9 copies	$5.95 each
10-49	$3.95 each
50 or more copies	$2.50 each
Shipping and Handling Charges	
If your order totals	Add
up to $5.99	$2.00
$6.00-$35.99	$4.00
$36.00-$149.99	$6.00
$150.00 and up	$10.00

FOR ORDERS SHIPPED OUTSIDE THE U.S. CONTACT THE
INFORMATION CENTERS FOR POSTAGE CHARGES.
PLEASE MAKE CHECKS PAYABLE TO
MADISON INSTITUTE OF MEDICINE.

Additional Booklets Available

In addition to *Attention-Deficit Hyperactivity Disorder in Children: A Medication Guide*, the following publications are available from the Madison Institute of Medicine Information Centers. The Centers can be contacted for current prices and order forms (see address page 51).

Antipsychotic Medications: A Guide. Jefferson JW, Temte JL, Greist JH. Information Centers, Madison Institute of Medicine, Madison, WI, rev. ed., 1998

Attention-Deficit Hyperactivity Disorder in Adults: A Guide. Johnston HF. Information Centers, Madison Institute of Medicine and Rockston Ink, Madison, WI, 2002

Carbamazepine and Manic Depression: A Guide. Medenwald JR, Greist JH, Jefferson JW. Information Centers, Madison Institute of Medicine, Madison, WI, rev. ed., 1996

Depression and Antidepressants: A Guide. Tunali (Şen) D, Jefferson JW, Greist JH. Information Centers, Madison Institute of Medicine, Madison, WI, rev. ed., 1999

Divalproex and Manic Depression: A Guide. Jefferson JW, Greist JH. Information Centers, Madison Institute of Medicine, Madison, WI, rev. ed., 2000

Electroconvulsive Therapy: A Guide. Barklage NE, Jefferson JW. Information Centers, Madison Institute of Medicine, Madison, WI, rev. ed., 2002

Fearful Flyer's Guide. Greist JH, Greist GL, Jefferson JW. Information Centers, Madison Institute of Medicine, Madison, WI, 1996

Lithium and Manic Depression: A Guide. Jefferson JW, Greist JH. Lithium Information Center, Madison Institute of Medicine, Madison, WI, rev. ed., 2001

Obsessive Compulsive Disorder: A Guide. Greist JH. Obsessive Compulsive Information Center, Madison Institute of Medicine, Madison, WI, rev. ed., 2000

Obsessive Compulsive Disorder in Children and Adolescents: A Guide. Johnston HF, Fruehling JJ. Obsessive Compulsive Information Center, Madison Institute of Medicine and Rockston Ink, Madison, WI, rev. ed., 2002

Oxcarbazepine & Bipolar Disorder: A Guide. Jefferson JW, Greist JH, Katzelnick DJ. Information Centers, Madison Institute of Medicine, Madison, WI, 2002

Panic Disorder and Agoraphobia: A Guide. Greist JH, Jefferson JW. Information Centers, Madison Institute of Medicine, Madison, WI, rev. ed., 2001

Posttraumatic Stress Disorder: A Guide. Greist JH, Jefferson JW, Katzelnick DJ. Information Centers, Madison Institute of Medicine, Madison, WI, 2000

Schizophrenia in Teens and Young Adults: A Guide. Johnston HF. Information Centers, Madison Institute of Medicine and Rockston Ink, Madison, WI, 2002

Social Anxiety Disorder: A Guide. Greist JH, Jefferson JW, Katzelnick DJ. Information Centers, Madison Institute of Medicine, Madison, WI, rev. ed., 2000

Trichotillomania: A Guide. Anders JL, Jefferson JW. Obsessive Compulsive Information Center, Madison Institute of Medicine, Madison, WI, rev. ed., 1998

Notes and questions